AF593639

14094

THE LAST DECADE OF GREAT WESTERN MAIN LINE STEAM

T. E. WILLIAMS

D. BRADFORD BARTON LTD

Frontispiece: No.4094 *Dynevor Castle*, from Stafford Road shed, at Norton Junction with a Worcester to Paddington train on 7 May 1955, still fitted with one of the original tall 'Castle' chimneys at this date.

ISBN 0 85153 282 9

printed in Great Britain by Thomson Litho Ltd, East Kilbride, Scotland
for the publisher

D. BRADFORD BARTON LTD · Trethellan House · Truro · Cornwall · England

foreword

As with most railway enthusiasts, my interest in steam trains started very early in life. My first memory of this at about five years of age, is of standing on the saddle of my tricycle to look over the bridge at Stratford-on-Avon station to see the trains passing by. By the age of about 15, watching them and noting down their numbers was not enough; I felt I had to record what I saw in picture form, particularly the larger express engines which interested me most.

Stratford, however, was not what I regarded as 'real' main line – for one thing, the 'King' class were not allowed through and even 'Castles' were infrequent until the Wolverhampton-Penzance services started to run again after the war.

The nearest point to what was undoubtedly main line, with 'Kings' and all, was Hatton, about eight miles away on the Paddington-Birmingham route. A wide variety of photographs could be obtained here, for the line went from embankment to a fairly shallow cutting with a nice S bend at the top of the bank, enabling one to get the sun in the right position for well-lit photographs for most of the day. All down trains had to work hard against the gradient, and some expresses needed assistance from Banbury or Leamington whilst most freight trains had a banker from Warwick.

Another good location on the Birmingham line was Harbury, a few miles out of Leamington towards London. Up trains had to do the hard work here, with a long curving climb on an embankment, past Fosse Road box then into a cutting curving towards Harbury tunnel. The London side of the tunnel was the most photogenic, particularly during the late afternoon. Down trains were more difficult to photograph and usually ran too fast for my shutters.

About ten miles south of Stratford the Paddington-Worcester line ran through Honeybourne and Chipping Campden providing an excellent stretch of line for photography. Up trains have a twisting climb here through wooded hillsides to Campden Tunnel. Worcester locomotives, particularly the 'Castles' shedded there were kept in immaculate condition in the mid 1950s, and the sight of one of these on the climb through the autumn-tinted trees to the tunnel was a sight never to be forgotten. Although trains were less frequent than on the Birmingham line the waiting was well worthwhile.

Another favourite stretch covering the Paddington-Bristol and South Wales line was around Challow and Wantage Road stations between Didcot and Swindon. Though the line was rather less picturesque, being virtually level and straight, the trains were so frequent that at times it was difficult to change films without missing something. The attraction here was the likelihood of ex-works locomotives resplendent in new paint being used on Swindon-Didcot stopping trains. Even 'Kings' and 'Castles' might be seen on these turns with two non-corridor coaches on.

Of course I journeyed much further afield; Twyford and Sonning cutting, Newton Abbot, Dainton, South Wales and elsewhere. The main difficulty in compiling this volume has been what to choose from out of the twelve thousand or so ex-GWR negatives which I took from lineside in the last decade of steam. The main lines remained always my favourite rather than the branches; alas, both have now gone for ever as we knew them.

Most of the photographs in this volume were taken with relatively inexpensive cameras (Agfa Record III, Rolfix II and Ikontas) using $3\frac{1}{4}$ x $2\frac{1}{4}$ roll film. Ilford FP3 or HP3 was normally used and over the years a variety of developing/enlarging materials were tried. The highest shutter speed all my early cameras were capable of was 1/500 sec and this was the limiting factor in 'stopping' fast expresses. For these, therefore, one had to 'pan' the camera in order to obtain a sharper image of the locomotive at the expense of background detail. As a point of interest I also on occasion fixed a 35mm camera to the larger one taking black-and-white, firing the shutters simultaneously to take colour transparencies at the same time.

The low winter sun flashes on the motion of No.6009 *King Charles II* as it hurries the 'Cambrian Coast Express' downhill towards Warwick on the run towards Paddington.

NAMED EXPRESSES . . . . .

Nearing the top of Hatton bank, a burst of exhaust from No.6010 *King Charles I* shows that she is being worked hard with the down 'Cambrian Coast Express' on 23 June 1959. This photograph was taken from the same location as the previous page, but looking in the opposite direction.

No.6017 *King Edward IV*, fitted with the first type of double chimney, in Sonning Cutting with the down 'Cornish Riviera' on 3 April 1956. To 'stop' this 70 mph train, the camera had to be panned, rendering the background slightly blurred.

The Paddington to South Wales 'Capitals United Express' threads the A4 road bridge in Sonning Cutting behind Landore 'Castle' No.5077 *Fairey Battle* on 4 August 1958.

CAPITALS
UNITED
EXPRESS
5077

THE
ROYAL DUCHY
150

The short-lived South Wales Pullman approaching Twyford on 31 March 1959 behind No.4093 *Dunster Castle*, one of the early 'Castles' in final form with double chimney and new inside cylinders.

No.6974 *Bryngwyn Hall* finds itself on top link work with the Paddington to Penzance 'Royal Duchy', again in Sonning Cutting, 7 September 1957. Some drivers say that a 'Modified Hall' in top condition had a job to be beaten.

Newton Abbot engine No.5024 *Carew Castle* heading for home with the down 'Torbay Express' in Sonning Cutting on 5 July 1955.

The fireman of No.5038 *Morlais Castle* appears to be having trouble with his fire as he approaches Dawlish Warren with the up 'Torbay Express', 9 August 1956.

The up 'Cambrian Coast Express' passing Fenny Compton behind No.6012 *King Edward VI*. The interesting array of signals is for the junction with the ex-SMJ single line to Stratford-on-Avon, enabling Banbury-South Wales freights to bypass Leamington Spa and Hatton bank. Below, One of the Laira stud of 'Kings', No.6025 *King Henry III*, lifts the up 'Cornish Riviera Limited' towards Whiteball Tunnel on 3 August 1956.

In typical Cardiff (Canton) condition, No.5030 *Shirburn Castle* accelerates past Scours Lane, Reading, with the down 'Capitals United Express' on 13 April 1957. Below, Looking very smart with its full set of chocolate-and-cream stock, No.6018 *King Henry VI* climbs away from Harbury Tunnel with the up 'Inter-City' on 14 May 1959.

No.7011 *Banbury Castle* speeds past Littleton and Badsey, near Evesham, with the down 'Cathedrals Express' serving Oxford, Worcester and Hereford.

Newton Abbot shed, short of locomotives, has had to provide 2-8-0 No.3840 for this S.O. Paignton to Nottingham train, seen passing Aller Junction on 13 August 1955.

4940
560 560

A credit to the cleaners at Worcester shed, No.7007 *Great Western* climbs away from Campden tunnel with an afternoon Hereford to Paddington train, 12 September 1957.

The 12.00 noon Penzance to Manchester leaves Dainton tunnel and starts its easy run down to Newton Abbot with No.4940 *Ludford Hall* and No.4090 *Dorchester Castle* in chargo, 2 September 1958.

5027
XO3

No.4977 *Watcombe Hall* lays a smoke screen across Barnwood sidings as it accelerates away from Gloucester with the Saturdays - only 8.30 a.m. Pembroke Dock to Birmingham (Snow Hill), 20 June 1959.

No.6016 *King Edward V* passing Rodbourne Lane box, Swindon, with a Paddington to Bristol express; 25 August 1957.

No.5027 *Farleigh Castle* passing Little Somerford with a South Wales to Paddington excursion, 14 May 1960. The all-maroon stock does not seem to suit the 'Castle'.

Overleaf, No.4088 *Dartmouth Castle* waits for the right away at Swindon with an up express from South Wales on a February day in 1957. The fireman takes advantage of the stop to trim his tender and pull some coal forward.

4088

5933

No.7005 *Sir Edward Elgar* hurries back home to Worcester after working the up 'Cathedrals Express'. The low camera angle was to avoid the exhaust covering the train as is likely with a north wind at this spot near Maidenhead; 8 April 1958.

Sporting a coat of new paint, No.5933 *Kingsway Hall* speeds past Twyford with an Oxford to Paddington train on 13 April 1957. The wind is blowing the exhaust over the train which normally was a disadvantage photographically but in this instance separates the bracket signal from the background.

Owing to engineering work on the main line on 24 May 1959, Paddington to Birmingham trains were diverted from Hatton to the North Warwickshire line, via Bearley. Here, the 2.10 p.m. Paddington to Birkenhead gently comes off the single line at Bearley and joins the Stratford-on-Avon to Birmingham line behind No.4090 *Dorchester Castle*.

With only 30 miles to Paddington, it was surprising to see this exhaust from No.6004 *King George III* as it approaches Twyford with the 7.15 a.m. Plymouth to Paddington on 13 April 1957.

600

925

No.6022 *King Edward III* pulls away from Leamington Spa, showing no signs of exertion, with the 4.10 p.m. Paddington to Birkenhead on 7 July 1959.

One of the few Oxford-allocated 'Castles', No.5012 *Berry Pomeroy Castle*, climbs towards Harbury Tunnel with a Birkenhead to Bournemouth train. The short chimney contrasts with that fitted to No.4094 on the frontispiece.

096

No.6019 *King Henry V* hurries through Lapworth with a Birkenhead to Paddington express. 2-6-2T No.8109 has worked a local from Birmingham and has reversed into the siding to allow the express to pass; later it will follow to Leamington as empty stock.

Stourbridge locomotive No.6803 *Bucklebury Grange* storms out of Stratford-on-Avon with an excursion to Weston-super-Mare. The halo of leaking steam helps to separate the engine from the cluttered background.

'Castle' No.5081 *Lockheed Hudson* can be heard a mile away at Honeybourne as she climbs the 1-100 Campden bank with a Sunday morning Worcester to Paddington train on 30 September 1956.

5031

With regulator closed, Cardiff (Canton's) famous No.5006 *Tregenna Castle* quietly runs through Severn Tunnel Junction station with a Paddington train on 4 October 1953. The diesel rail car on the left has worked an enthusiasts special from Birmingham.

Diesels having displaced the 'Kings' at Laira, No. 6026 *King John* now works from Old Oak Common and is seen passing Kings Sutton, near Banbury, heading for home with a 13-coach 'Cambrian Coast Express' in 1962, minus headboard.

A rare occurrence on the Birmingham route; 2-8-0 No.4704 on Hatton bank with a relief to the down 'Cambrian Coast Express' on 23 August 1958.

With the low evening sun reflecting on the smoke box door, No.6014 *King Henry VII* climbs Hatton bank with the 5.10 p.m. Paddington to Wolverhampton. This locomotive has a special bracket on its inside cylinder cover for attaching the reporting number frame as this could not be carried on the smokebox door when it had the 'bullet nose' streamlining.

Sunday p.w. work on Hatton bank has diverted No.6012 *King Edward VI* to the goods loop and is seen here approaching Hatton station to rejoin the main line with a Paddington to Wolverhampton excursion on 27 October 1957.

185

No.5035 *Coity Castle* on a down Bristol train in Sonning Cutting directed to the relief line during p.w. work; 19 February 1955.

No.4084 *Aberystwyth Castle* in Sonning Cutting with an up Bristol express; 19 April 1954.

FREIGHTS . . . . .

Running downhill from Harbury tunnel towards Leamington, No.4707 looks quite smart for a freight engine. What a pity this class never had copper-capped chimneys!

The 47xx were favourites for night fitted freights and were rarely seen in daylight hours. No.4703 from Bristol is seen here heading an up freight through Wantage Road Station.

No.6912 *Helmster Hall* approaching Wootton Bassett on the South Wales line with an up mixed freight, 14 May 1960.

An unusual locomotive for freight working, No.1025 *County of Radnor*, entering Shrewsbury station with an up freight. The tracks curving off to the right lead to Crewe.

No.2805 has difficulty in starting its train of empty iron ore tipplers out of Stratford-on-Avon on 23 April 1958. The Collet 0-6-0 on the extreme left is waiting to bank it to Wilmcote.

With distant 'on', No.3800 coasts slowly south through Stratford-on-Avon with a mixed freight for Gloucester.

Descending Hatton bank Banbury Mogul No.5332 heads for its home shed with a freight from Honeybourne on 17 March 1956. This locomotive has one of the few 'intermediate' tenders which was larger than usual for Moguls.

Veteran rebuild No.4900 *Saint Martin* going well up Hatton with a Banbury to Cardiff fitted freight on 16 February 1957. Visible detail differences from this engine and the rest of the 'Halls' was the shorter steam pipes and the lack of brass beading round the splashers.

On a bright crisp March morning No.4178 accelerates away from Hatton with a train of empties for Leamington. Ideal conditions for train photography, low but bright winter sun and the cold air enhancing the exhaust.

No.3836 trundles its southbound freight through Wilmcote station near Stratford-on-Avon on 16 February 1957. Again, the cold winter sunshine has helped to produce a 'cotton wool' exhaust.

No.8100 near Harbury tunnel with a local pick-up freight from Leamington. This particular locomotive has the frames of the original 2-6-2T prototype No.99 of 1903. Renumbered to 3100 in 1912, it was rebuilt and renumbered 5100 in 1929 and finally was rebuilt again and renumbered 8100 in 1938.

A 38xx 2-8-0 hurrying towards Cardiff with a fitted freight on the down main line out of Newport meets No.4203 on the up slow with a train of oil tanks in May 1957. Below, On the same day, No.3803 near Pontypool Road with a coal train.

No.4079 *Pendennis Castle* has steam to spare as she approaches Standish Junction, south of Gloucester, with a short freight consisting of old locomotive boilers for Swindon – its home shed at the time – summer 1962.

Looking very smart with its polished copper trimmings and new lined green paintwork after a visit to Caerphilly Works, No.5619 from Barry shed passes Severn Tunnel Junction with a freight for the Gloucester line, July 1959.

IRONSTONE TRAINS . . . . .

Banbury Mogul No.5361 climbs towards Harbury Tunnel with a train of iron-ore empties from South Wales.

2878

No.2878 running through Lapworth station with a Banbury to Croes Newydd iron ore train in April 1958. The two tracks in the foreground are the up and down relief lines which terminate here.

0-6-2T No.6671 passing Kings Sutton with a stone train to Banbury, summer 1962.

Ex-R.O.D. No.3028 struggles up the goods loop on Hatton with an iron-ore train from Banbury. The new brickwork on the overbridge shows where it collapsed during heavy rain the previous winter.

PARCELS AND MILK . . . . .

Swindon shed seldom seemed to set a very good example for cleanliness; grimy No.5023 *Brecon Castle* hurries through Challow with an embarrassing load of one van and brake for Banbury.

On a warm summer evening in 1956,no sign of exhaust can be seen from No.4061 *Glastonbury Abbey* as she tops Hatton bank with the Paddington to Shrewsbury parcels.

A rather dirty No.1012 *County of Denbigh* from Swindon passing Hinksey yard at Oxford with an up parcels train in 1963.

No.5006 *Tregenna Castle* approaching Newport with a train of empty parcel vans for Old Oak Common.

Overleaf: Because of a collision at Leamington Spa on 25 February 1957, all Birmingham to London trains were diverted via Stratford-on-Avon and Oxford. No.7819 *Hinton Manor* from Oswestry on an up parcels train coasts through Stratford, showing a good head of steam.

4949

More milk empties going west, this time passing Didcot on 16 August 1960 behind Gloucester engine No.7003 *Elmley Castle*.

No.4949 *Packwood Hall*, from Taunton, returning west with the Kensington to Penzance empty milk tanks – a photograph taken in Sonning Cutting on 11 June 1957.

Overleaf: the 12.30 p.m. Penzance to Kensington milk train climbs to Dainton summit behind No.5967 *Bickmarsh Hall* and 2-8-0 No.3834 on 30 August 1958.

No.4909 *Blakesley Hall* with a Banbury to Oxford local passes under the Aynho flyover which carries the main line from Paddington via High Wycombe.

5101

Banbury to Princes Risborough auto train leaving Kings Sutton behind No.1440. The auto coach is named *Thrush.*

eader of the class, No.5101 in smart green lined livery leaves Stratford-on-Avon with a eamington to Worcester stopping train on 5 July 1959.

6979

No.6979 *Helperly Hall* heads out of Leamington with a one-coach local for Banbury on 2 March 1957.

5813

Another Leamington to Stratford local, this time on Hatton bank behind No.7702, also showing GWR on its panniers, 6 May 1953.

Leamington Spa to Stratford-on-Avon local leaves the Birmingham main line at Hatton ıd takes the sharp curve to Stratford. Note the fixed distant. 0-4-2T No.5813 is still ttered GWR in May 1957!

8109

No.8109 again, seven years later, sporting a new coat of black paint and working a local from Birmingham approaching Lapworth.

No.8109 on a Leamington Spa to Birmingham train passing Hatton outer home signal, 2 April 1956. This locomotive was a rebuilt from No.5115 in 1939 with smaller wheels and higher boiler pressure. Allocated to Leamington, together with No.8100, these were favourites for banking duties from Warwick to Hatton.

No.4094 *Dynevor Castle* emerging from the Severn Tunnel with a Cardiff to Bristol stopping train on 18 September 1959.

It was unusual to see a pannier tank with express headlamps but No.9482 was doing a good turn of speed on the down main line south of Newport with this unidentified train of non-corridor coaches on 18 May 1957.

9482

The driver of No.5933 *Kingsway Hall* has just shut off steam for the stop at Chipping Campden with a Worcester to Oxford train on 12 September 1957.

No.2222 has been on banking duties all day at Honeybourne and here has charge of an evening Moreton-in-Marsh local, photographed as it approaches Campden tunnel in August 1963.

No.6152 gets away from Twyford with a Reading to Paddington train on 19 April 1954. This sight was so common that it was rarely considered worth photographing.

EXCURSIONS AND SPECIALS . . . . .

No.7013 *Bristol Castle*, masquerading as No.4082 *Windsor Castle*, climbs Hatton bank with the Royal Train, May 1962. Information regarding the destination of this train was restricted by BR security.

Collett 0-6-0 No.2203 near Hatton North Junction heading a steam breakdown crane towards Birmingham on 23 March 1957.

Harbury Tunnel, one of my favourite locations. The cooler air in the tunnel helps to show up the exhaust of No.4997 *Elton Hall* on a Wolverhampton to Newbury race special on 10 April 1954.

A Paddington to Birmingham football special on Hatton bank behind No.6015 *King Richard III* which shows the original style of double chimney. The cold March air has enhanced the exhaust and the wind has blown it away from the camera, separating the locomotive from background trees.

Unusual task for *City of Truro;* an Inspectors' saloon going south near Evesham Road crossing, Stratford-on-Avon on 8 September 1958.

013

Another down Birmingham football special on the same day; No.5014 *Goodrich Castle* does not seem in a hurry as it approaches the top of Hatton at about 20 mph with steam in hand.

Westbury shed usually provided a clean locomotive for the 12.30 p.m. Paddington to Weymouth. No.4917 *Crosswood Hall*, having worked up to London earlier in the day, is now working back home on the slow line in Sonning Cutting on 19 February 1955.

No.5084 *Reading Abbey* heading towards London, near Moreton Sidings at Didcot, 14 April 1955.

Overleaf: a few yards to go to Dainton Summit yet the driver of No.1015 *County of Gloucester* is confident enough not to have his hand on the regulator which appears to be only half open, but is enough to lift a ten coach Paignton to Plymouth return excursion over the top.

D
X
1015
COUNTY OF GLOUCESTER

No.2844 heading east out of Newport with a train of empty iron-ore wagons, 18 May 1957.

Running-in after a visit to Swindon works, No.6026 *King John* leaves Wantage Road station with a stopping train to Didcot in September 1960.

Another running-in turn, No.7019 *Fowey Castle* easily accelerates its two coaches away from Challow on the way back to Swindon from Didcot, September 1960.